# Simply Believe

## Trusting God's Promises for Conception & Delivery

By

Kathy Hicks

This title *"Simply Believe"* is a revision of *"Facing the Giant of Unbelief Concerning Conception"* written by Kathy Hicks which was originally published in 2017.

ISBN 13: 978-0-578-59045-5   (Paperback)

All scripture references from KJV Bible

All rights reserved. No part of this publication may be reproduced, distributed, or transmitted in any form or by any means, including photocopying, recording, or other electronic or mechanical methods without the prior written permission of the publisher. For permission requests, solicit the publisher via the address below.

Believing His Word Ministries

P.O. Box 694

Tontitown, AR 72770

www.believinghiswordministries.com

Email: Kathy@believinghiswordministries.com

# Dedication

First, I want to thank God for blessing me to be able to write this book. It is intended to be all for His honor and glory.

To my husband, Lloyd, I want you to know how very much I love you and am so thankful for the thirty-two years of marriage that God has blessed us with. I pray that we will have many more to come!

To our children, Brandon, Brent, Bryson, Brooke, and Braden, there will never be words to express how thankful that I am to God for allowing me to be blessed with you!

It has always been my desire to raise you all for His honor and glory. Most of the time, I have felt like I have failed miserably at that task. God knows my heart, and I hope that you do too. My prayer for you all is that you will grow closer to Him each day and that you will always love each other.

I also, want to extend a very special thank you to our oldest sons, Brandon & Brent for helping to revise this book!
Without your amazing talent and skill I wouldn't have been able to self-publish. With their help, this book is now what I envisioned from the start!

# Introduction

My story is one of having a tubal reversal; however, I believe that anyone can stand on God's promises and conceive no matter what your circumstances might be!

I have had the awesome opportunity for the past fifteen years to reach out to many women who for whatever reason were having issues conceiving. I could never even start to count or even

> *"Prayer is the best weapon we have." (Toby Mac)*

remember for that matter how many books (Jackie Mize, *Supernatural Childbirth*) and personal letters that I have given or sent to these women.

In April (2016), as I sat preparing two books to send out, God impressed upon me that I should write my on book! I have never had that feeling before. I truly know that it was God's prompting in my life! My heart's desire is to reach as many women as God would have me to.

I get so excited every time that I have the opportunity to try and encourage someone else! I want them to hang on and not give up before God is ready to bless them. I want you to know that there is hope!

The most important thing that I got from Jackie's book is to *simply believe*! I read it several times before I actually got it! I have prayed over those years to somehow be an encouragement and a help to others facing the same path that I have been down.

God continues to bring new people my way, and I am so thankful for that! We could never praise Him enough for what He has done and continues to do in our lives! The road isn't always easy, but God is so faithful and loving. He will never leave or forsake His children.

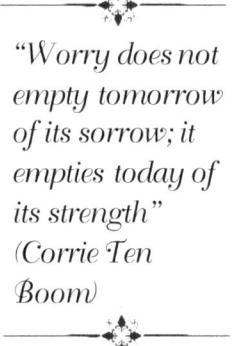
*"Worry does not empty tomorrow of its sorrow; it empties today of its strength" (Corrie Ten Boom)*

We have learned through many trials that through our struggles, God is able to work in wonderful ways, and it is all for His honor and glory.

I have prayed over every word in this book and asked God to write it through me that you might be encouraged and find the strength in Him to continue on your journey. Follow God's prompting in your life and always know, "With God ALL things are possible" (Matthew 19:26).

# My Story

When I was in elementary school, God blessed me with a very special friend. Her name was Angela, and at the time, I did not realize what an impact her friendship would have on my life.

My parents did not attend church. I had never gone to church before, other than an occasional vacation Bible school during the summer that someone invited my sister and me to.

They focused mainly on cares of the world. They both worked full-time jobs and were always struggling to pay bills and meet the needs of our family.

*"Don't underestimate what God is doing in your season of waiting." (Toby Mac)*

They didn't have a good relationship and fought often, which led to great amounts of stress and bitterness.

My sister, who is four years older than me, and I spent a lot of time alone. We were not very close, with the age difference. When she reached high school, she found things to keep her busy and was not at home very often.

I truly do not know where I would be today if God had not brought Angela into my life! She was a sweet friend, and we sometimes would spend time together after school just playing and talking about different things.

She was an only child with godly parents who had taken her to church and taught her about God and salvation and how she should share it with others. I am so thankful for their witness and that God chose to bring them into my life! Angela told me about Jesus who died on the cross so that I might be saved.

I did not know anything about God or Jesus or even about the free gift of salvation! John 3:16 says, "For God so loved the world, that he gave his only begotten Son, that whosoever believeth in him should not perish, but have everlasting life."

I realized while writing this that I didn't have a Bible at that time! How wonderful it would have been if I could have read God's promises and known His truths! I am so thankful that now I can read His word and find comfort no matter what I am going through. Psalms 119:105 says, "Thy word is a lamp unto my feet, and a light unto my path." God is faithful, and if we truly seek Him, He will never leave us or forsake us!

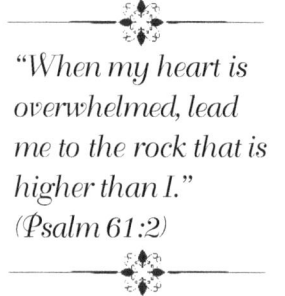

*"When my heart is overwhelmed, lead me to the rock that is higher than I." (Psalm 61:2)*

I began to pray every morning and every night that Jesus would save me. Being a child and not knowing anything about God, I just continued to pray, hoping that God would hear me and save me! I also prayed for my family for their salvation and that my parents would start taking us to church.

I truly believe that when we are faithful to pray without ceasing, that God is faithful in hearing and answering our prayers in His Perfect time! The key to that phrase is "In HIS perfect time" not ours. Psalms 27:14 says, "Wait on the Lord: be of good courage, and he shall strengthen thine heart: wait, I say, on the Lord."

Everything that happens in our lives can only be if God allows it. It is hard at times to see what God is doing, but He always has a plan! Trials are to make us stronger and to draw us closer to Him. 2 Corinthians 12:9 says, "And he said unto me, My grace is sufficient for thee: for my strength is made perfect in weakness. Most gladly therefore will I rather glory in my infirmities, that the power of Christ may rest upon me."

God heard my prayers, and after about a year, my mother started taking my sister and me to church!

Prayer is such an important thing in my life. Sometimes, God answers quickly, and other times, I just need to be still and accept that He has a perfect plan and that He knows what is best. Psalms 46:10a says, "Be still and know that I am God." Philippians 4:6–7 says, "Be careful for nothing; but in everything by prayer and supplication with thanksgiving let your requests be made known unto God. And the peace of God, which passeth all understanding, shall keep your hearts and minds through Christ Jesus."

After we started attending church I went forward to make a profession of faith. I prayed with my pastor the prayer of salvation, but I truly believe that God saved me when Angela first witnessed to me! Romans 10:9–10 says, "That if thou shalt confess with thy mouth the Lord Jesus, and shalt believe in thine heart that God hath raised him from the dead, thou shalt be saved. For with the heart man believeth unto righteousness; and with the mouth confession is made unto salvation."

Through the years of junior high and high school, I continued to grow closer to God. I tried to learn as much as I could about how He wanted me to live. Our home life continued to be a mess, and most of the time, I felt so alone and unloved, but I knew that God loved me and I wanted so much to live for Him!

I met my husband, Lloyd, in high school. He came from a broken home where neither of his parents went to church. I invited him, and he began to go with me. Not long after he started going, he accepted Christ as his savior! I had been praying for quite some time for God to lead me to the one that He had prepared for me, and as time went on, I knew that Lloyd was the one!

We were married April 18, 1987, and we both wanted to establish a home built on God's word. We struggled as most young couples do. We were trusting God to meet our needs, and He always has!

Many mistakes were made along the way, but God has always so graciously helped us and blessed us beyond anything we could have ever imagined! With our first pregnancy in December of 1988, I suffered a miscarriage. Then in January of 1989, we were blessed with a second pregnancy. Two weeks past my due date, we went to the doctor's office and found out that I had developed toxemia. I was rushed to the hospital for and emergency C-section. The surgery went well, and we had a healthy baby boy! Brandon Lloyd was born on October 27, 1989.

After Brandon was born, I had issues with postpartum. My husband was such a blessing to me.

He stayed by my side, taking care of me and Brandon.

In between Brandon and our next baby to be born, I suffered another miscarriage. Brent Roger was born on September 11, 1991.

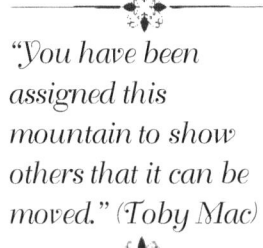

*"You have been assigned this mountain to show others that it can be moved." (Toby Mac)*

With the complications of my first pregnancy and delivery, we, along with my doctor, decided that another C-section would be best.

While I was pregnant with Brent, we made the decision, on our own, to have a tubal ligation after the baby was born.

Looking back over time, I have tried to remember if we prayed at all about what God would have us to do in that situation. If we had only known to search the scriptures and find out how God felt about us having children, things could have been very different. We were thinking about our own feelings and what we thought would be best for our family.

I don't remember at the time feeling convicted about having it done, but I can certainly tell you that I had a huge conviction about a year or so after Brent was born. I wanted another baby, and I was so sorry for making such a bad decision.

The desire continued to get stronger as the years went by. I was praying for God to take the desire from me if it wasn't his will. I just knew that God would never forgive me for being so selfish and having the tubal ligation done. That was just another lie from the devil to keep us from trusting God. He will forgive our mistakes or sins; however, we still have to deal with the consequences. If we are faithful to follow His plan, He is more than able to give us the desires of our heart according to His will! The Bible says in 1 John 1:9: "If we confess our sins, he is faithful and just to forgive us our sins, and to cleanse us from all unrighteousness."

God has never broken a promise, yet all too often we listen to the voices of doubt and refuse to act upon what God has told us in His word. Every word in the Bible is inspired by God, and if He says it, then we can believe it! Hebrews 11:6 says, "But without faith it is impossible to please him: for he that cometh to God must believe that he is, and that he is a rewarder of them that diligently seek him."

We have been given the word of God and the Holy Spirit, but often we ignore that awesome resource and look for some other kind of guidance for living. God's still, small voice can easily be drowned out by the world if we do not listen intently for Him.

I tried for about eight years after Brent was born to accept the fact that we had two wonderful children, and because of our careless decision, we would never have anymore. God, however, had other plans for our life! I wanted more children so bad that I could hardly stand it, and that desire was not going away!

We began to get information on having a tubal reversal. All the while praying for God's direction and seeking His will. The first big issue with the surgery was that it was not covered under our insurance.

I have always stayed at home with our children, and Lloyd only made a modest income at that time. Our needs were always met, but we definitely did not have extra money, especially for a surgery that we didn't have to have!

I didn't know how, but I knew that God would meet our needs if we earnestly prayed, ask for forgiveness, and trusted Him! 2 Corinthians 5:7 says, "For we walk by faith, not by sight." I didn't need to know how, I just needed to trust Him!

We prayed for over a year, and then God met our need! We called and scheduled the surgery and had it done on February 26, 1999.

It was amazing to see how God had worked to supply our needs! I was nervous, but I knew that God would keep me safe, and I truly felt that it was His will to have the surgery done.

We didn't have any support from our families. We felt like it was our little family of four against the world! God had blessed us with good Christian friends in our church who supported us and that were praying with us. Hebrews 12:1 says, "Wherefore seeing we also are compassed about with so great a cloud of witnesses, let us lay aside every weight, and the sin which doth so easily beset us, and let us run with patience the race that is set before us."

*"To love God is to love his will. It is to be content with His timing and wise appointment."*
*(Elisabeth Elliot)*

I am so thankful for the godly people that God continues to place in our lives to encourage us and lift us up before the Lord!

After the surgery, we were so hopeful that soon, we would have another precious baby on the way. Several months went by and we had a positive pregnancy test! As with each pregnancy after a tubal reversal, as soon as you have a positive test, you go to your doctor to have an ultrasound to ensure that the baby is in the uterus and that all is well.

I went and had the ultrasound and assumed that everything was fine only to get a phone call the next day, saying that my pregnancy was ectopic. The baby was stuck in my fallopian tube, and the doctor wanted to do an emergency surgery to remove both the tube and the baby. I could hardly believe what the doctor was saying.

The only other option was to have a shot of methotrexate to dissolve the baby. An ectopic pregnancy, if not taken care of, will most likely result in death for the mother. I was devastated.

I started to pray and ask God for direction. After a few hours, we decided to go with the shot to try and save the tube. I cannot even start to express how scary the situation was, but I knew that God was in control. I can only say that we were at peace with that decision and it felt right.

I have learned over the years to pray for God's conviction in a mighty way if I shouldn't do something.

I'm sharing this with you now so that you don't have to learn the hard way like I did with the tubal ligation.

If you have had a tubal ligation, please don't think that it's the end concerning your having another baby! God is still on His throne and He's still in control of all things! He is more than able to meet your needs, whatever they might be, and He is more than willing to meet you where you are to make it happen!

A wise man once said, "The farther we are willing to go and the bigger the sacrifices that we are willing to make … will result in the biggest blessings that we receive!"

With having the shot, I had to go in once a week for six weeks to have my blood drawn to make sure that the pregnancy levels were going down because there was a possibility of the shot not working. We had waited for so long for this precious baby and then had to make the choice to dissolve it.

There are no words to describe the pain in our hearts and in times like this, God is certainly our comfort and strength.

Even with going through all that we had, I still had a mighty peace in my heart that God would bless us with another child in His perfect time. Isaiah 40:31 says, "But they that wait upon the Lord shall renew their strength; they shall mount up with wings as eagles; they shall run, and not be weary; and they shall walk, and not faint."

After the ectopic, a friend told me about Dr. Berger at Chapel Hill Fertility Clinic. She was praying for the funds to have a tubal reversal, and she had been researching about him for some time. (Another one of those times that God placed the person in my life that I needed!)

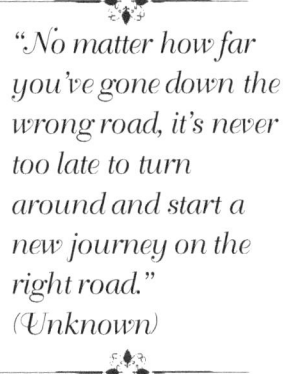

*"No matter how far you've gone down the wrong road, it's never too late to turn around and start a new journey on the right road."*
*(Unknown)*

The first thought in my head was after all that we have been through, I couldn't bear the thought of another surgery, much less could we afford another surgery!

She said that sometimes the first surgery wasn't successful and that I might need to have more repairs made. At this point, I realized that I wasn't having the faith in God that I had when I started the journey!

We all go through times of doubt. I wasn't really doubting that God would bless us with another child, I just wanted to make sure that He really wanted me to have another surgery!

I truly know and believe that all things are possible through Christ, and I surely believed that if it was His will that He could just heal me without the surgery, and I was definitely praying for that!

I think having faith in Him requires us at times to show Him that we are willing to go where He is leading us!

For me, it was to have another surgery. We were believing that He had brought us this far and He could certainly see us through! Giving up was not an option, but we still didn't know how in the world it was going to happen!

My first step was to move forward with finding out about this new doctor, so I pulled up his web page and was very impressed by what I saw.

The surgeon who did my first reversal was not interested at all in trying to help us any further. We had an HSG test at the hospital after the ectopic, and it showed that my right tube was partially blocked. After he got the results, he called me on the phone and gave me no hope at all. When I questioned him further, he replied, "You will never bring another baby home from the hospital."

He said that if I was fortunate enough to become pregnant, that it would be ectopic and that I would lose my tubes. I can't explain how I felt at that moment, but somehow, I had peace and I knew that my God was in control and that I would have another baby in His perfect time!

Little did I know that at the same time that I was dealing with my ectopic, my dear friend Angela who now lives about an hour or so from me, was also dealing with a miscarriage. Somehow, God allowed her to find out what was happening with me, and she called to comfort me and to tell me about a book that someone had shared with her! The book was *Supernatural Childbirth* by Jackie Mize! It was the exact encouragement that I needed to continue my journey!

I want to interject here the importance of choosing the right doctor to do your tubal reversal or anything related to fertility! If we had only had the right information and advice, our road could have been much smoother! Just because a surgeon might be less expensive or closer to home doesn't make him or her the best person for the job.

Dr. Gary Berger specialized in tubal reversals, and although we had to travel for more than two hours, we knew after reviewing his web site and speaking with his staff that it was exactly where we needed to go!

We knew above all else that we first sought God's will and direction, and He gave us peace that this was the place to go!

When we went, the center was Chapel Hill Tubal Reversal Center. It has now been moved from Chapel Hill, North Carolina, to Raleigh, North Carolina, with the same staff that are so wonderful to work with! Dr. Charles W. Monteith is now the surgeon who does the reversals.

In 2008, he began a training mentorship under Dr. Gary Berger. (Please see their web page at www.tubal-reversal.net where you will find a wealth of information.)

We were amazed at how far people would travel to be able to have Dr. Berger do their reversals! I can certainly tell you from our experience that it was more than worth the effort and expense.

Now on to how God would meet our needs for this to happen!

We made an appointment for a free consultation, drove two-plus hours, met with Dr. Berger, and knew this was God's plan for us!

*"Many of life's failures are people who did not realize how close they were to success when they gave up." (Thomas Edison)*

I will never forget driving home. It seemed more like five hours coming back. I cried the entire way. My husband felt so defeated. We wanted to have the surgery so badly, and neither of us could see how God would meet our need.

I know that the devil takes every opportunity to lead us into depression, worthlessness, and just a total lack of hope. Isn't it so wonderful that God is always in control and He will never leave us!

Please don't listen to the lies of the devil. If God has placed this desire in your heart, He is more than able to meet your needs and see you through! It makes no difference whether you are facing a reversal or any procedure or even if you just haven't been able to conceive at all. Matthew 19:26 says, "But Jesus beheld them, and said unto them, 'With men this is impossible; but with God all things are possible.'"

You have to keep putting one foot in front of the other and trusting Him to clear your path. Again, we walk by faith, not by sight!

The next week was very long for us. We prayed harder than we ever had before! Our Christian friends were praying with us, but I could sense that they were starting to doubt God's plan for our life. One even said to me, "Maybe it's just not God's will for you to have more children."

I know that the devil meant that for discouragement, but I didn't say anything to her. I just thought, *You will see what God does with this situation.*

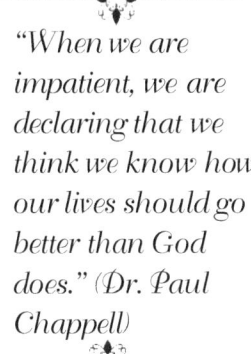

*"When we are impatient, we are declaring that we think we know how our lives should go better than God does." (Dr. Paul Chappell)*

I don't know God's plan for your life or how long it might take for Him to meet your needs, but exactly one week later, He met our need for the second surgery!

Little did we know, but certain friends of ours had been praying that week too and they called to offer us the exact amount that we needed, $6,500!

I could hardly believe what I was hearing over the phone.

They were expecting a baby at that time, and they wanted us to have the money, but they also wanted to make sure that we could pay it back over time.

My heart sank, and I thought, *Oh my goodness! We can't tell these people, who are our friends, that we can definitely pay this amount back anytime in the near future!*

When I hung up the phone, Brandon, our oldest son, said to me, "Mama, you know that we prayed specifically that if it wasn't God's will or if we wouldn't be able to pay the money back, that we wouldn't get it."

I can't even start to tell you how that made me feel. My child was having more faith than I was at that moment. We had been praying that if it wasn't God's will, that we wouldn't get the funds for the surgery.

When our needs were met in such an unexpected way, we were able to trust that it was definitely His will and that He would see us through whatever lay ahead.

I am so thankful for the prayers of our children! They just pray and simply believe.

Of course, we accepted the money and scheduled the surgery! I couldn't explain the peace that I had, but I knew that God was in control and He was meeting our needs.

It's always hard when you know that you can't just give up, but the unknown of what lies ahead is so scary. Isaiah 41:10 says, "Fear thou not; for I am with thee: be not dismayed; for I am thy God; I will strengthen thee; yea, I will uphold thee with the right hand of my righteousness."

My second reversal surgery was done on August 16, 2000. On the morning of the surgery, everything was going well. As the last preparations were being made to go into the surgery room (this is a personal clinic, so it's much more simple than a big hospital with an operating room), which is also a lot more comforting by the way, all of a sudden, I started to panic. The devil certainly didn't want me to go through with this surgery.

The nurse stepped into the next room to get my husband and our two sons. She knew that I needed to see them and that they would be comforting to me. I looked up at them and said, "Pray for me."

At that moment God sent an amazing peace over me! I was able to go in and get on the operating table, knowing that I was in the center of God's will for my life!

After the surgery when Dr. Berger came in to talk to us, he said the surgery went well, but that he had to remove my right fallopian tube because it was so mangled from the first reversal surgery.

He said that the left fallopian tube had become twisted after the first reversal surgery and had stuck to something else. By sticking, it had remained twisted and didn't have a clear path for an egg to travel through. The left tube was in good condition, so he had straightened it out and made sure that it was clear. He also wrapped it in something to make sure that it would stay straightened out going forward.

We were so thankful to have that news, and although I only had one fallopian tube left, we knew that it would be enough according to God's will for us to conceive again! Psalms 100:4 says, "Enter into his gates with thanksgiving, and into his courts with praise: be thankful unto him, and bless his name."

We certainly were praising God for blessing us and meeting our needs and also for giving us the strength to continue moving forward! Psalms 46:1 says, "God is our refuge and strength, a very present help in trouble."

I wish I had documented my journey more at the time and would now have a more specific time line with all the dates in order.

I am so thankful for God inspiring me to write down at least all that I can remember.

It was a couple of months after the second surgery that we had a positive pregnancy test! Again, we were so excited only to find out a few days later that I had miscarried.

I don't know why, but for some reason, I thought that God was telling me that everything was okay, it just wasn't time yet.

As we continued to pray and trust God, It certainly wasn't an easy road. I cried often and wondered why God wouldn't just bless us with a baby.

Looking back now, I know that He was working His plan in our lives and growing our faith and trust in Him.

I wouldn't take anything now for the lessons that we have learned along the way. The trials taught us how to trust God in so many other areas of our life, and with each new trial that we have faced, we have become so much stronger in Him. Psalms 34:18 says, "The Lord is nigh unto them that are of a broken heart; and saveth such as be of a contrite spirit."

At this same time, we were going through purchasing a house to add to our stress.

The very week of moving into our new home, we made the last payment on the money that was loaned to us for the second surgery! We were so thankful, and at that point, we had no idea how we were able to do it so quickly! The entire $6,500 was paid in less than a year. Another huge weight had been lifted off our shoulders and we were excited to see what God had in store!

I am so happy to tell you that six weeks after moving in to our new home, we had another positive pregnancy test!

That was on Friday and on the following Monday, my husband had to have emergency eye surgery for a torn retina.

With being on our own (no family support), it was very stressful for me. The hospital was about an hour from our home. Friends from church helped take care of Brandon and Brent while I drove back and forth to the hospital.

The day after Lloyd's eye surgery, I began spotting and was so afraid that I might lose the baby. I called a friend, who was actually the person that told me it might not be God's will for me to have more children.

She drove to the hospital to pick up Lloyd because he was being discharged that day.

When she got him home, she then went with me to the ob-gyn to be evaluated. I prayed the whole way there that everything would be fine, but I was also preparing for the worst.

I know that my friend had to be feeling so sorry for me. We didn't speak hardly at all on the ride to the doctor's office.

Lloyd had gone with me all the times before, but this time, he wasn't able and going back for the ultrasound, I just remember feeling so nervous.

As soon as the ultra sound technician started looking, she said, "The baby is up high in the uterus right where it's supposed to be!" I'm not sure at that point which one of us was happier because she had done all of my ultrasounds and we were both afraid to look!

It felt like my heart might burst! I could hardly wait to tell Lloyd and also my doubting friend in the waiting room!

*Faith- It does not make things easy, it makes things possible." (Luke 1:37)*

I think maybe God led me to call her for help so that He might show her just how mighty He is! Psalms 103:17–18 says, "But the mercy of the Lord is from everlasting to everlasting upon them that fear him, and his righteousness unto children's children; To such as keep his covenant, and to those that remember his commandments to do them."

Over the next couple of days, the spotting stopped. I had morning sickness all day long, and it was okay because we now had a strong pregnancy!

With all that we had been through, we were so thankful for each new day that things were still going well and all was well with the precious baby that God had chosen to bless us with! Psalms 127:3 says, "Lo, children are an heritage of the Lord: and the fruit of the womb is his reward."

On February 5, 2002, we arrived at the hospital for a scheduled C-section very early in the morning. It still felt like a dream. We could hardly believe our baby would soon be here!

Brandon and Brent were now ten and twelve years old, and they were excited to meet their baby brother. My surgery went well, and Bryson Mark was finally here.

We felt so blessed beyond anything we could have ever imagined. We knew in our hearts that we certainly wanted more children if God chose to bless us with more in the future. Psalms 127:4–5 says, "As arrows are in the hand of a mighty man; so are children of the youth. Happy is the man that hath his quiver full of them: they shall not be ashamed, but they shall speak with the enemies in the gate."

On the very morning that we brought Bryson home from the hospital, we immediately typed out an e-mail with pictures attached and sent it to the surgeon that had done my first tubal reversal. We had been waiting for some time to be able to tell him because he had told me specifically that I would never bring another baby home from the hospital.

I don't think even thirty minutes passed until I heard Lloyd on the phone giving information to someone about our new baby. It was the surgeon calling to find out all the details!

I hope he realized on that day that only God knows what He has in store for those that place their trust in Him.

Please don't ever let anyone tell you that anything is impossible. Keep going until you find someone who is willing to help you! Pray for God's direction, and He will lead you right where you need to be.

Sometime after Bryson was born, I became pregnant again and suffered another miscarriage. We continued to trust God for another child, and in His perfect time, we had another baby on the way!

I could hardly wait for the time to come for my ultrasound! My heart longed for a precious baby girl and I truly hoped that this baby would be just that!

I was truly thankful for my boys, and if this baby was a boy, then I would be thankful, although I really had a strong desire in my heart for a girl.

Just to have a healthy baby was such a blessing from God. But to have a girl would be totally awesome! I tried to prepare myself for another boy, but when the technician said, "It's a girl!" I almost shouted!

Another person came in to look a few minutes later and we didn't tell him what the first technician said. He also said that it was a girl!

On July 1, 2003, Brooke Katherine was born by a scheduled C-section.

I couldn't believe that God had blessed us with such a perfect and beautiful baby girl. I pray for my daughter that she will treasure this verse and grow into the godly young woman that God would have her to be: "Favour is deceitful, and beauty is vain: but a woman that feareth the Lord, she shall be praised" (Proverbs 31:30).

After Brooke, I had another miscarriage and then became pregnant with our fifth child to be born. We were very thankful to have another healthy baby on the way!

Braden James was born on April 17, 2006, the day before our nineteenth wedding anniversary and it was the best gift we could have ever imagined!

Psalms 37:4–5 says, "Delight thyself in the Lord; and he shall give thee the desires of thine heart. Commit thy way unto the Lord; trust also in him; and he shall bring it to pass."

Braden is now thirteen years old, and all of those trials seem like a lifetime ago. With all that God has taught us through those trials, we wouldn't change one thing!

The principles that we have learned have helped us with so many other trials along our way.

God has always been faithful in His perfect time to bless us and more than meet our needs! We still make mistakes, however growing in God is a lifelong process.

We still go through times of not having faith in God as we should and then we quickly ask for forgiveness.

You would think after all of those lessons we would not have times of doubt. I'm so thankful that God never gives up on me! Numbers 14:18a says, "The Lord is longsuffering, and of great mercy, forgiving iniquity and transgression."

I truly hope that through the sharing of our trials, you might be encouraged to continue on your journey. Ephesians 6:10–11 says, "Finally my brethren, be strong in the Lord, and in the power of his might. Put on the whole armour of God, that ye may be able to stand against the wiles of the devil."

*"Do not ask God to guide your footsteps… If you're not willing to move your feet." (Sean Patrick Flanery)*

Scripture to me is so precious. The verses are God's promises to us, and I find the more I read them, the stronger I am in Him. If you knew me personally, you would know that I am definitely not a strong person . . . without God! Psalms 28:7 says, "The Lord is my strength and my shield; my heart trusted in him, and I am helped: therefore my heart greatly rejoiceth; and with my song will I praise him."

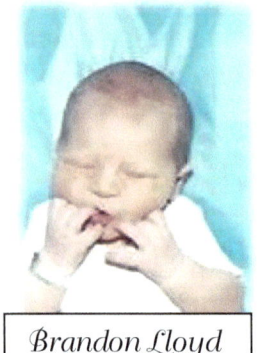
Brandon Lloyd

Brent Roger

Bryson Mark

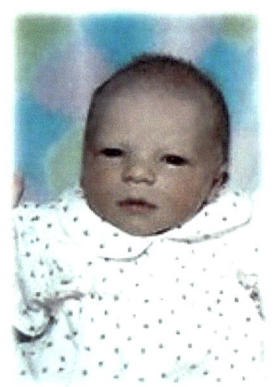
Brooke Katherine

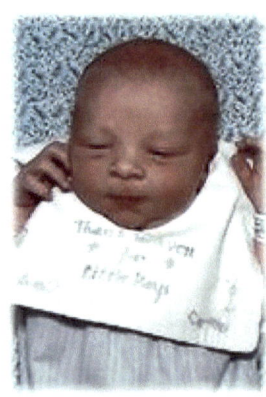
Braden James

# Testimonies

I knew before I even started writing this book that I wanted to include some testimonies from others who have gone down different paths to eventually arrive at the same destination, having their hearts desire!

My hope is that through their sharing of their journeys, you might also be encouraged.

We all have different stories, but in the end, God has kept His promises, and we have beautiful babies to love and cherish and to raise for Him.

Psalms 113:9 says, "He maketh the barren woman to keep house, and to be a joyful mother of children. Praise ye the Lord."

Thank you to Jessica and Amy for being so willing to share your journey and for being a blessing to others!

# Jessica

*Todd and Jessica Batterton*
*They have two sons, Gabe is 4 and Asher is 1.*

I have dreamed of being a mom from the time I was a little girl. Unfortunately, once I became a teenager, it became obvious something was wrong.

I didn't officially find out that I have PCOS until I was about twenty-seven, but I had friends who also had it and I already had that gut feeling.

I was put on some medication to help with the PCOS and advised to eat well and exercise. So I did. And I prayed. I prayed all the time. Every time, it entered my thoughts.

And the months rolled by. Those months turned into years. Sometimes, there were months that my hopes were so high that I believe I must have tricked my mind into thinking I was pregnant. I'd think, *Oh, I'm late, I'm nauseous, etc. I may be pregnant!*

*Simply Believe*

Then a few weeks later, my hopes came crashing down with my next cycle. It was a great thing that my cycles were actually becoming regular, but it's hard to be happy for that when all you want is a baby.

So I continued on that roller coaster of extreme highs then extreme lows until December 2014.

My pastor preached a message on Hannah, and I know God had that message just for me.

I finally gave it completely to God, laid it all at His feet—I was done with letting it control my life. That was no way to live life, especially if that wasn't what God had planned for me. I wanted to want what He wanted for me. So that's what I prayed for, "Make my desires Your desires, Lord."

That next year, on February 5, we found out I was pregnant and welcomed our baby boy into the world on October 6, 2015. God truly has blessed us!

*Todd and Jessica also have another son on the way and he is due to be born in December, 2019!*

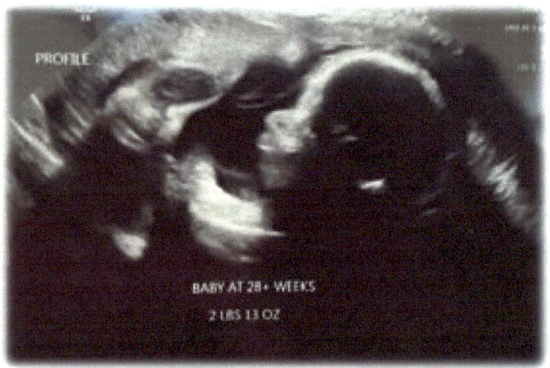

*Finley Cade Batterton*

*Simply Believe*

*Sam and Amy Scott*

*They have two sons, Emmett who is five & Zane is three and a daughter, Anna who is one!*

"He maketh the barren woman to keep house, and to be a joyful mother of children. Praise ye the LORD" (Psalm 113:9).

I did not doubt that God could make me a mother, but would He?

"And they that shall be of thee shall build the old waste places: thou shalt raise up the foundations of many generations: and thou shalt be called, The repairer of the breach, The restorer of paths to dwell in" (Isaiah 58:12).

As a young girl, I had a burden and desire long before I even had a faithful and godly husband.

Isaiah 58 is addressing Israel, but God is always true to His Word. Verse 12 has been my burden and my promise. The breach is my burden, the restoration is my promise, but without children, what could His plan possibly be for me? Why would He give me such a strong desire for children and then withhold them from me? Why did He close my womb when there were those who had children and were not grateful? Why would He give me a wonderful, supportive husband who also wanted to make a difference in this world and desired children and not make him a father? Why would He place us in a church where the home and family were the burden of the Pastor's heart and not give us a family to raise there?

The first year is considered "normal." The second year I had begun to wonder why, and by the third year, I knew something must certainly be physically wrong with me. The fourth, fifth, and sixth year of my infertility, I learned to trust and

*"Never be afraid to trust an unknown future to a known God." (Corrie Ten Boom)*

understand the sovereignty of God knowing He could and would make me a mother.

He taught me truths from His Word that otherwise may have never been realized. He gave me peace and comfort in the place that hurt deep within me that no one, no matter how sincere or well meaning, could ever touch. He gave me genuine joy, and He gave me a heart full of contentment rather than bitterness and I watched as He fulfilled the promises He had revealed to me from His Word. "Trust in the LORD, and do good: so shalt thou dwell in the land, and verily thou shalt be fed" (Psalm 37:3).

The Lord was feeding me with His Word, and whenever I would sorrow, whenever I would doubt, I could dive into His Word, I would find His promises, and I would cling to them and not let go.

"Delight thyself also in the LORD and He shall give thee the desires of thine heart" (Psalm 37:4). My heart's desire was children. I delighted in the Lord, so where were my children? I desired children in order to bring Him glory to be as arrows in the hand of a mighty man.

In my heart, my motives were pure; surely now He would open my womb! But His Word cleansed my mind and humbled me; the still small voice, always true to God's Word, said, "What if you being childless is what I want to bring me glory?" Oh, the goodness of the Lord!

He began to give my heart a new desire from Him. I watched as His truth was revealed. "He shall give thee the desires of thine heart." He gave my heart the desire to bring Him glory, here, now, in this moment, through this trial, in this place! There were springs in the desert He was leading me through.

"Commit thy way unto the LORD; trust also in him: and he shall bring it to pass. And he shall bring forth thy righteousness as the light, and thy judgment as the noonday" (Psalms 37:5–6).

There was healing taking place in my heart because of His Word. His truth gave me true joy for others who were expecting. I can testify that it was Him alone who gave me joy for others who received what I longed for deeply. There was not the slightest bit of sorrow or jealousy in my heart as there had been when I would hear of another woman expecting a child. Only God can do this because that joy is not indicative of human nature.

"Rest in the LORD, and wait patiently for him: fret not thyself because of him who prospereth in his way, because of the man who bringeth wicked devices to pass" (Psalms 37:7).

Infertility tends to heighten your sensitivity, and you notice those who seemingly have the ideal family yet squander their lives, forsake their children, and prosper despite their sin.

Worse still is the normalcy of abortion and the hardened heart people can have concerning abortion. Here I was desiring to bring forth life, and there are those who are quick to extinguish life simply for the sake of their own convenience. I had to learn not to fret despite these things, and though I continue to mourn the loss of innocent lives, I cannot allow that to consume me or steal my joy.

"Cease from anger, and forsake wrath: fret not thyself in any wise to do evil. For evil doers shall be cut off: but those that wait upon the LORD, they shall inherit the earth" (Psalms 37:8).

Early in the journey I wondered, What did I do? Am I being punished? God's Word tells us that we are guilty; all are guilty of sin (Romans 3:23). But His Word also reveals that our circumstances and trials are not always a punishment.

Our bodies are wounded and scarred by sin, sometimes even from sins we commit but also because death and decay are a part of this world. We bear in our bodies the result of the sin that entered the world by Adam. But that was not God's desire for us. He did not desire that we would have these mortal, imperfect bodies; His plan for us is perfect communion with Himself. He desires it so much that even with the result of sin being death, He made a way though His perfect Son to restore us so that we will spend an eternity with Him. That restoration is a process, and we must wait patiently for His coming.

I realized that if I allow bitterness and regret to take hold in my heart because of sin that has been forgiven, it would rob me of the joy that I have in this life. I had to allow the washing of the water of the Word to cleanse me, as its truth reaps joy and contentment in my heart.

This world does not need to see defeated Christians. They need to see the victory we have only in Christ despite the marks of sin we still bear in our bodies. It is because of the hope we have in Christ that we can have any hope at all through our temporal circumstances.

I did have hope for healing, but several factors left me undiagnosed for many years, and I struggled with the idea of medical intervention.

We were not in a position financially to be able to pursue the infertility treatments that would more

*"You don't have to be afraid of the unknown. It is unknown only to you. God is well aware of where you are and of every step he is asking you to take." (Unknown)*

than likely be recommended for us, and adoption was not something we were able to pursue either, although we did pray about it, knowing the Lord is able to provide.

When I had an opportunity to pursue medical help for my infertility, I did proceed with the intention of being a good steward of my body and to find out what was physically wrong. I felt that by knowing the physical problem, perhaps I could also learn how to be a better steward of my body.

Tests revealed my body's inability to ovulate and the immediate recommendation of the doctor was to induce ovulation.

My sincere prayer through the entire process was that if it was not God's will for me to have children at this time, my womb would remain closed.

After three months of failed attempts to medically induce ovulation, I was referred to a specialist whose office ended up contacting me to reschedule. In so many ways, I was relieved for at that time, we were moving. I told them I would contact them at a later date to possibly reschedule, but I knew that their recommendation would not be for healing but would be medically induced conception, and that was not a desire that we had. I did not hinge my hope or my happiness on medicine or what doctors could or could not do for me.

We had faith in the Great Physician and His current prescription was infertility, and my desire was to trust that process and He who "worketh in me both to will and to do of his good pleasure" (Philippians 2:13).

I will interject that I am thankful for modern medicine and do not feel that there is necessarily anything wrong with pursuing medical help or intervention as it can also be a blessing and a tool available, but for us at that time, it was not the right thing.

I think the greatest treasure I found is learning to share in my Savior's sorrow. Infertility hurts and often feels like a lonely road to travel even though you know so many experience infertility and have been where you are. Isaiah 46:3–5 says, "Hearken unto me, O house of Jacob, and all the remnant of the house of Israel, which are borne by me from the belly, which are carried from the womb: And even to your old age I am he; and even to hoar hairs will I carry you: I have made, and I will bear; even I will carry, and will deliver you. To whom will ye liken me, and make me equal, and compare me, that we may be like?"

My desire for children can never compare to the desire He has for His children. I cannot for a moment think that He does not know what sorrow I bear in my heart. He has us, we are His, and yet our hearts can so often be far from Him. How it must break His heart to not be able to hold the children that are already His. I never want to be that child; I never want any distance between us. We may have an eternity with Him in heaven, but there is so much here, and now He wants us to know that He longs to show us.

Realizing the longing that He has for me and others that are His ignited a fire in me. It caused me to count it a privilege to be in this place, and I thanked Him sincerely for my infertility. "I bring near my righteousness: it shall not be far off, and my salvation shall not tarry: and I will place salvation in Zion for Israel my glory" (Isaiah 46:13).

The following are my notes from church services on our seventh wedding anniversary:

Sunday, March 10, 2013, Sunday school

"The Peril and Perplexity of Faith" (Joshua 6:1–3)

Nothing can come to the child of God except by the hand of God. Will you obey the Lord or not? God is scriptural; he will not lead his people away from the principles of his Word. God told Israel what to do. There is safety in following God's will for our lives, even if that "will" seems perplexing.

Sometimes, when you think nothing's happening, that's when everything is happening. It happens in obedience, simplicity, sincerity, and standing during the perplexing times.

What you will suffer from the world—criticism, celebration. Get ready to be misunderstood. Faith may at times have to experience disaster. God is secure in himself. You're engraved on the palms of his hands; God is secure, and he is sovereign.

## Sunday Morning

"Faith—what is it?" Hebrews 10:38.

The just shall live by it. Faith is to believe what we do not see, and the reward of this faith is to say what we believed. Faith is not just knowing that he can but that he will. Faith sees the invisible, believes the incredible. These just give us the reality of faith, but not exactly what it is.

What we learn in chapter 11 is preceded by what we have already learned in chapter 10—God wants us to give and by faith, not by works. God has never let us down; he will not let you down, for he cannot let you down. Faith is action, present tense, a continual action; substance—substructure, essential; things hoped for—expectations, the object of our faith, of our hope; evidence–proof, a certain persuasion; of things—facts, deeds, works. Faith is based on fact—the transaction of what has been done in my heart. Not seen—ability, we are able to see because we trust.

1. My salvation is based on faith—you cannot take it any other way (John 3:16).

2. Faith is necessary for us to believe. Faith is necessary for one to trust. When God says he is going to do something he will do it (Acts 16:30–31). The doing has been done; we put our faith in what the Lord Jesus Christ has done for us. This is the only way.

3. My service is based on faith (Hebrews 11:7). In Ephesians 2:8–9 Noah did what God said and only because he said it—not because he understood what he was doing, for he had never seen an ark before. Vs 8 obedience—the only way to show that you believe. Vs 9–10, 17, he walked when he did not know where he was going. I believe God for it, and he did it. When God calls you, he is going to support you. Faith enables us to serve God.

4. My stability is based on faith. Stability comes by knowledge; we must submerge ourselves in God's word. Faith cometh by hearing and hearing by the word of God. Memorize the word of God, echo the word of God, live the word of God, practice the word of God, use the word of God, and live it out. Hebrews 11:6 talks about growing in grace. Stability is calm assurance. Doubt sees the obstacles; faith sees the way.

On our way out of church that morning, our pastor greeted us with a knowing look in his eyes. I said, "I don't just know that He can. I know that He will."

Fast forward fifteen weeks, my husband and I are sitting in a doctor's office. As she looks at a prediction calendar, she informs us, "We have no way of knowing if these are entirely accurate, but I think it's always fun to know! Based on your measurements, it says here the date of conception would be around March 11."

As I sat down to write out my testimony to share with you, I started by opening His Word to revisit all of those springs He had shown me and realized that the verse preceding my promise has always said there would be a drought! How did I even miss that?

"And the LORD shall guide thee continually, and satisfy thy soul in drought, and make fat thy bones: and thou shalt be like a watered garden, and like a spring of water, whose waters fail not. And they that shall be of thee shall build the old waste places: thou shalt raise up the foundations of many generations: and thou shalt be called, The repairer of the breach, The restorer of paths to dwell in" (Isaiah 58:11–12)

It is such a joy to see His Word and His truth come alive in my own heart and life. Always have faith, always have hope, and always know that His longing for you is far beyond any longing you could ever have.

    Seek to know Him, the power of His resurrection and the fellowship of His sufferings (Philippians 3:10–14). For there you will find His amazing love for you and the perfect peace and contentment that only His love can bring through any and all of life's circumstances.

# Stand on God's Word and Be Strong in Him

*Romans 12:2*: "And be not conformed to this world: but be ye transformed by the renewing of your mind, that ye may prove what is that good, and acceptable, and perfect, will of God."

*First John 5:14*: "And this is the confidence that we have in him, that, if we ask any thing according to His will, he heareth us."

*Psalms 37:4–5*: "Delight thyself also in the Lord; and he shall give thee the desires of thine heart. Commit thy way unto the Lord; trust also in him; and he shall bring it to pass."

*Psalms 127:3–5*: "Lo, children are an heritage of the Lord: and the fruit of the womb is his reward. As arrows are in the hand of a mighty man; so are children of the youth. Happy is the man that hath his quiver full of them; they shall not be ashamed, but they shall speak with the enemies in the gate."

*Psalms 128:3*: "Thy wife shall be as a fruitful vine by the sides of thine house: thy children like olive plants round about thy table."

*Deuteronomy 7:13–14*: "And he will love thee, and bless thee, and multiply thee: he will also bless the fruit of thy womb . . . Thou shalt be blessed above all people: there shall not be male or female barren among you."

*Exodus 23:26*: "There shall nothing cast their young, nor be barren, in thy land: the number of thy days I will fulfil."

*Ephesians 3:20*: "Now unto him that is able to do exceeding abundantly above all that we ask or think, according to the power that worketh in us."

*Romans 12:2*: "And be not conformed to this world: but be ye transformed by the renewing of your mind, that ye may prove what is that good, and acceptable, and perfect, will of God."

*John 15:7*: "If ye abide in me, and my words abide in you, ye shall ask what ye will and it shall be done unto you."

*Proverbs 6:2*: "And this is the confidence that we have in him, that, if we ask any thing according to his will, he heareth us: And if we know that he hear us, whatsoever we ask, we know that we have the petitions that we desired of him."

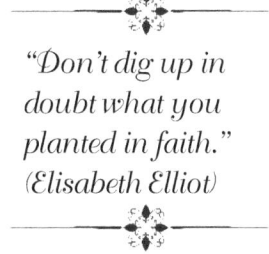

*"Don't dig up in doubt what you planted in faith."*
*(Elisabeth Elliot)*

*Deuteronomy 30:19*: "For verily I say unto you, That whosoever shall say unto this mountain, Be thou removed, and be thou cast into the sea; and shall not doubt in his heart, but shall believe that those things which he saith shall come to pass; he shall have whatsoever he saith."

*Philippians 4:13*: "I can do all things through Christ which strengtheneth me."

*Philippians 4:19*: "But my God shall supply all your need according to his riches in glory by Christ Jesus."

*Luke 1:37*: "For with God nothing shall be impossible."

*Psalms 113:9*: "He maketh the barren woman to keep house, and to be a joyful mother of children. Praise ye the Lord."

# Additional Scripture

I also want to give you some scripture to read when the devil is trying hard to discourage you and even trying to make you be fearful of what lies ahead on your journey. Always remember that God is in control and you are never alone!

*Second Timothy 1:7*: "For God hath not given us the spirit of fear; but of Power, and of Love, and of a sound mind."

*Psalms 56:3*: "What time I am afraid, I will trust in thee."

*Psalms 56:11*: "In God have I put my trust: I will not be afraid what man can do unto me."

*Romans 8:15*: "For yea have not received the spirit of bondage again to fear; but yea have received the spirit of adoption, whereby we cry, Abba Father."

*Isaiah 41:10*: "Fear thou not; for I am with thee: be not dismayed; for I am thy God: I will strengthen thee; yea I will help thee; yea I will uphold thee with the right hand of my righteousness."

*Psalms 23:4*: "Yea, though I walk through the valley of the shadow of death, I will fear no evil: for thou art with me; thy rod and thy staff they comfort me."

*Psalms 27:1*: "The Lord is my light and my salvation: whom shall I fear? The Lord is the strength of my life: of whom shall I be afraid?"

*John 14:27*: "Peace I leave with you, my peace I give unto you: not as the world giveth, give I unto you. Let not your heart be troubled, neither let it be afraid."

*"The circumstances we ask God to change are often the circumstances God is using to change us." (Max Lucado)*

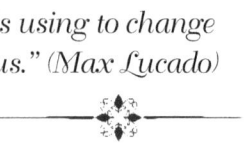

*Proverbs 3:21-26*: "My son, let not them depart from thine eyes: keep sound wisdom and discretion: so shall they be life unto thy soul and grace to thy neck. Then shalt thou walk in thy way safely, and thy foot shall not stumble. When thou liest down, thou shalt not be afraid: yea, thou shalt lie down, and thy sleep shall be sweet. Be not afraid of sudden fear, neither of the desolation of the wicked, when it cometh. For the Lord shall be thy confidence, and shall keep thy foot from being taken."

*Psalms 103:17-18*: "But the mercy of the Lord is from everlasting to everlasting upon them that fear him, and his righteousness unto children's children; To such as keep his covenant, and to those that remember his commandments to do them."

*Psalms 23:1*: "The Lord is my shepherd; I shall not want.

Be encouraged and keep your eyes on God. He will meet you where you are and bring you where you need to be!

# Plan of Salvation

If you are reading this book, there is a desire in your heart to conceive and have the precious gift that can only come from God!

In order to stand on His promises and be able to receive that precious gift, you first must be born again. I am praying for every person who reads this book that if you haven't already, you will receive the perfect gift of salvation and be able to trust God to give you the desires of your heart!

*Romans 3:23*: "For all have sinned, and come short of the glory of God."

*Romans 5:8*: "But God commendeth his love toward us, in that, while we were yet sinners, Christ died for us."

*Titus 3:5*: "Not by works of righteousness which we have done, but according to his mercy he saved us, by the washing of regeneration, and renewing of the Holy Ghost."

*Ephesians 2:8–9*: "For by grace are ye saved through faith; and that not of yourselves: it is the gift of God: Not of works, lest any man should boast."

*Romans 6:23*: "For the wages of sin is death; but the gift of God is eternal life through Jesus Christ our Lord."

*Romans 10:9–10*: "That if thou shalt confess with thy mouth the Lord Jesus Christ, and shalt believe in thine heart that God hath raised him from the dead, thou shalt be saved. For with the heart man believeth unto righteousness; and with the mouth confession is made unto salvation."

*John 3:16–17*: "For God so loved the world, that he gave his only begotten Son, that whosoever believeth in him should not perish, but have everlasting life. For God sent not his Son into the world to condemn the world; but that the world through him might be saved."

If you truly believe these promises from God's word, here is a prayer that you might pray for your own salvation:

Lord Jesus, I know that I am a sinner and I do not deserve eternal life. But I believe You died and rose from the grave to make me a new creation and to prepare me to dwell in your presence forever.

Jesus, come into and take control of my life, forgive my sins, and save me. I am now placing my trust in You alone for my salvation and I accept your free gift of eternal life.

Amen

# About the Author

Kathy is the mother of five children who range in age of thirteen to thirty and has been married to her high school sweetheart for thirty-two years. Along with homeschooling her children, she also helps her husband with their family business.

For sixteen years, they have owned a safety consulting business, which takes them across the United States to do training for their customers.

With their travels, she frequently encounters women who are struggling with infertility for many different reasons.

It is her heart's desire to encourage and inspire others to keep going on their journey to having their hearts desire!

She accepted Jesus Christ as her personal savior when she was eleven years old and feels that she will never stop growing and learning to be more like Him.

She is thankful that God led her to write this book, not only to hopefully encourage others, but also to leave as a legacy of faith for her children.

She feels that raising her children to live for God is the most important task that God has given her and she wishes to finish well!

www.ingramcontent.com/pod-product-compliance
Lightning Source LLC
Chambersburg PA
CBHW041812040426
42450CB00001B/5